CRAZY CAT LADY

CRAZY CAT LADY

Agnes Loonstra & Ester Scholten

Workman Publishing • New York

Library of Congress Cataloging-in-Publication Data is available.

ISBN: 978-1-5235-0557-9

Illustrations by Agnes Loonstra
Text by Ester Scholten

Design by Kat Millerick

Workman books are available at special discounts when purchased in bulk
for premiums and sales promotions as well as for fund-raising or educational
use. Special editions or book excerpts can also be created to specification.
For details, contact the Special Sales Director at the address below, or send
an email to specialmarkets@workman.com.

Workman Publishing Co., Inc.
225 Varick Street
New York, NY 10014-4381
workman.com

WORKMAN is a registered trademark of Workman Publishing Co., Inc.
Printed in China
First printing February 2019
10 9 8 7 6 5 4 3 2 1

crazy cat lady

(n) \krā-zē kat lādē\

1. <u>archaic:</u> twentieth century for an older single woman who lives alone with a large number of cats, to which she is obsessively devoted.

2. A person who knows how amazingly awesome cats are and owns at least one.

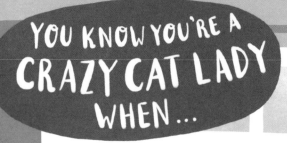

PET STORE

ANIMAL SHELTER

7 Your favorite locations around town are cat-related

CAT CAFÉ

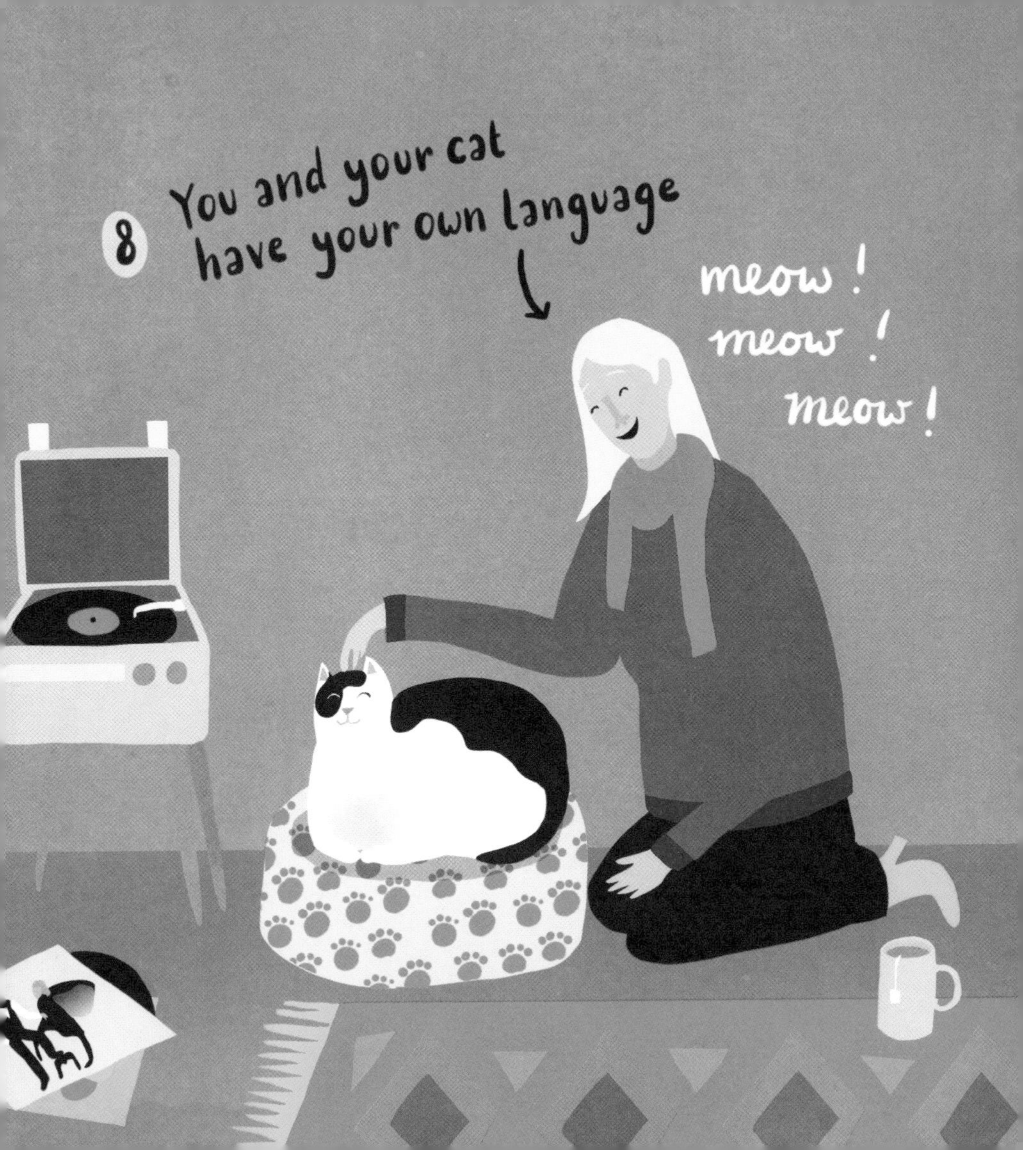
8
You and your cat have your own language
meow!
meow!
meow!

YES,
I really need
all these cats.

It's <u>not</u> drinking alone when the cats are home.

There are many breeds of crazy cat lady...

I don't need THERAPY, I talk to my CATS.

#instanthappiness

YOU KNOW YOU'RE A **CRAZY CAT LADY** WHEN...

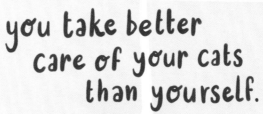

you take better care of your cats than yourself.

Did I groom myself during the last two hours?
YES
NO
NO
let's groom!
YES
Let's take a nap!
Am I hungry?
YES
NO
nom nom nom!
Have I pushed something off the table today?
NO
find a random object and push it off the table
YES

FAMOUS CAT LADIES

→ CHER

the
BRONTË
SISTERS

AUDREY
HEPBURN

HALLE BERRY

TAYLOR SWIFT

KATY PERRY

IF I FITS, I SITS.

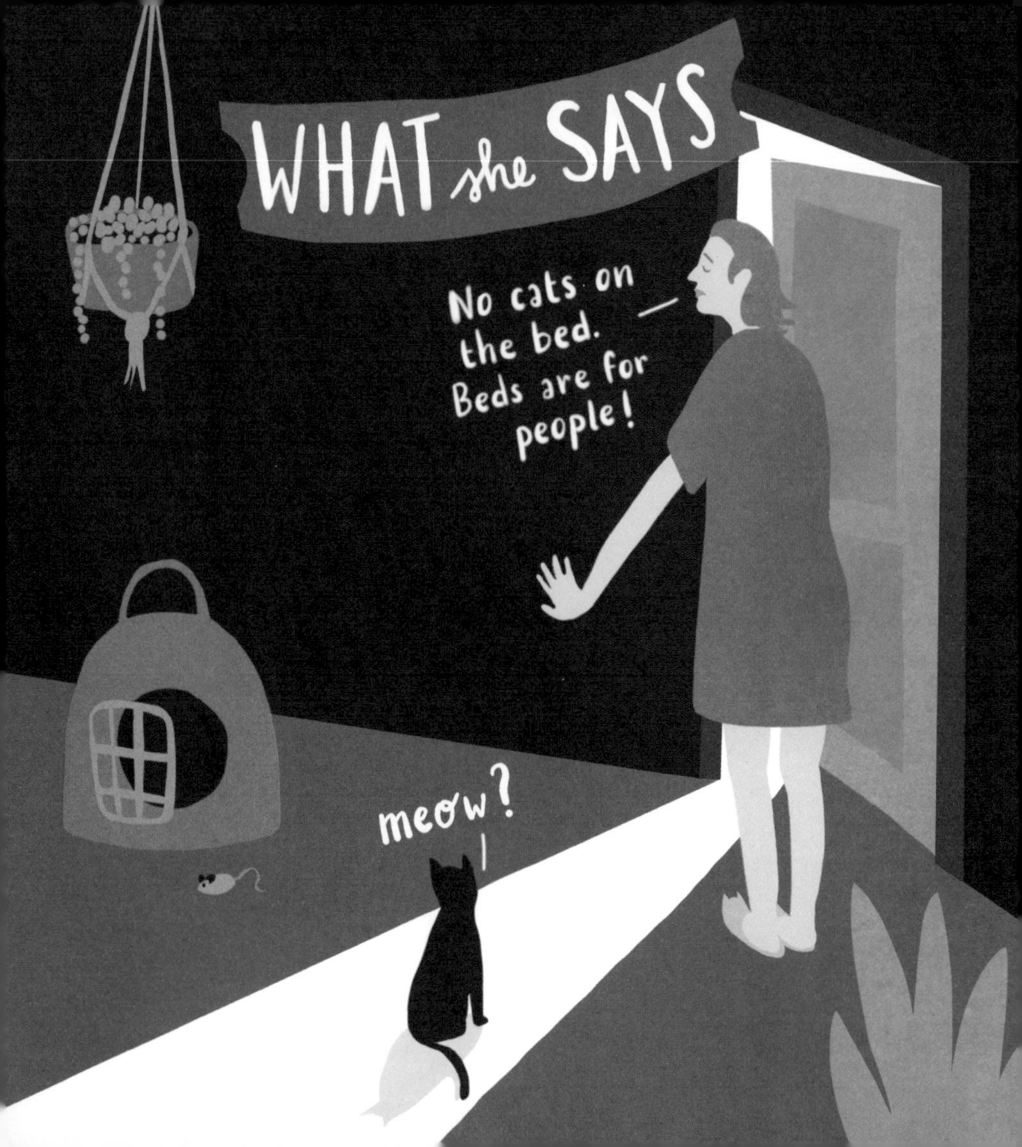
WHAT she SAYS
No cats on the bed. Beds are for people!
meow?

WHAT she DOES

I was NORMAL three cats ago.

I LOVE CATS

YOU KNOW YOU'RE A CRAZY CAT LADY WHEN...

you own at least three items with cats on them

DO I NEED ANOTHER CAT?

START

YES

NO

Do you already have more than 3 cats?

MANEKI NEKO

↳ Japanese good luck charm

Left paw up attracts customers

Right paw up attracts good fortune and money

How to

MAKE THE PERFECT CAT TOY

1 GRAB A TAMPON FROM YOUR BAG.

2 REMOVE PLASTIC.

first real meow

First BDAY

Baby's Firsts

first time going potty

First hair ball

you

complete

me.

CATS ARE LIKE
GLASSES OF WINE—

YOU
CAN'T
HAVE

JUST
ONE.

"But all cats, bless you, have much more sympathy and feeling than human beings have."

—Florence Nightingale, founder of modern nursing and owner of about 60 cats during her lifetime

YOU KNOW YOU'RE A **CRAZY CAT LADY** WHEN...

your friends are worried about your social life.

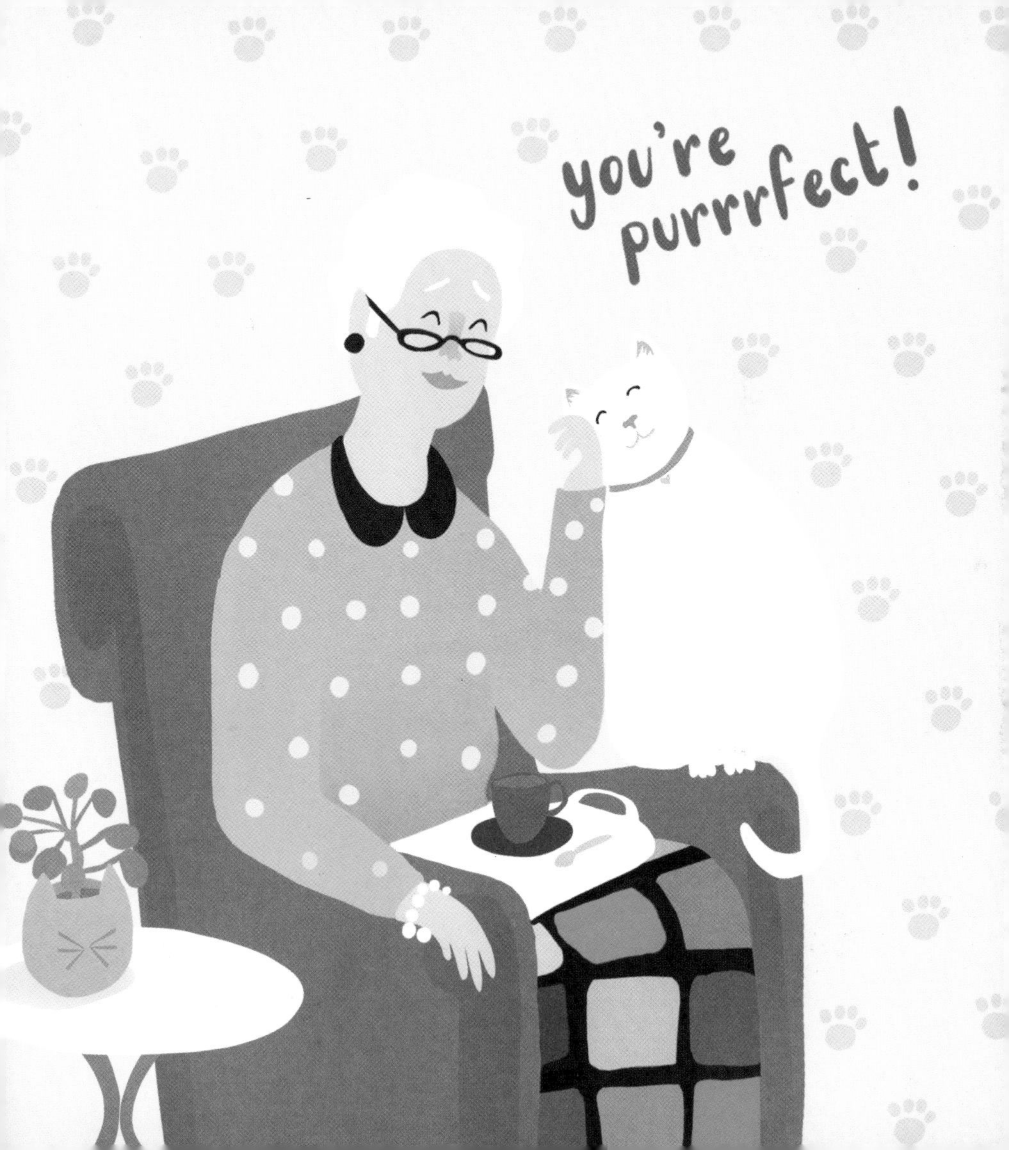
you're purrrfect!

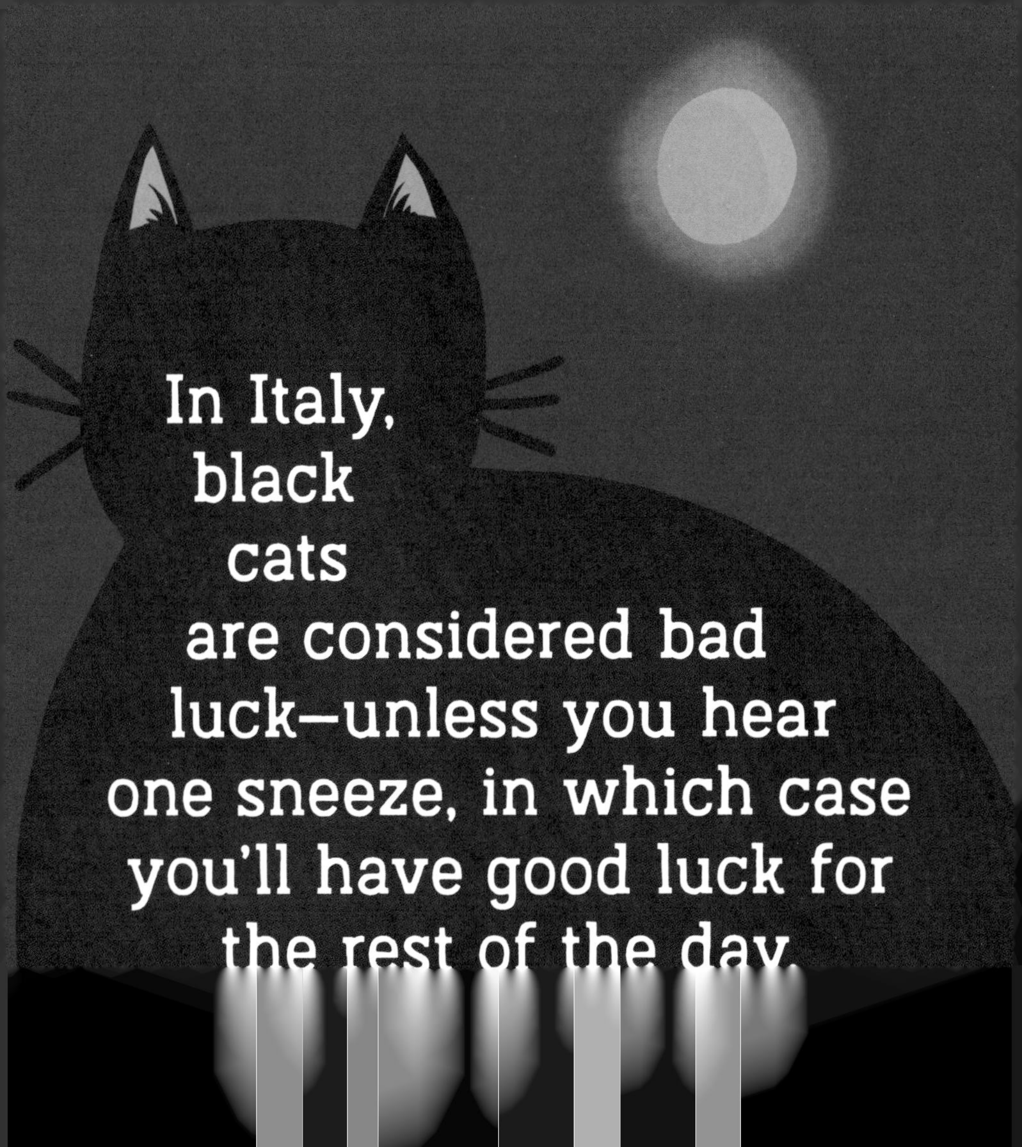

In Italy,
black
cats
are considered bad
luck—unless you hear
one sneeze, in which case
you'll have good luck for
the rest of the day.

What should you name your cat?

Sushi
Oreo
cereal
pasta

Do you like FOOD?

Are you VERY literal?

Cat
Mr. Meow
Kitty

Are you a MUSIC lover?

Cat Stevens
Madonna
Elvis

Obama
Buddha
Jane Fonda

Do you have a QUIRKY family member?

Uncle Harry
Buddy
Granny

Have you always dreamed of having CELEB friends?

Inch
Pixel
Pi

Are you a math GEEK?

Do you like OTHER animals?

Are you the ULTIMATE crazy cat lady?

Tiger
Panda
Turtle
Whale

Mittens
Sugar
Bubbles

HOME IS WHERE the CAT IS.

YOU KNOW YOU'RE A CRAZY CAT LADY WHEN...

YOU HAVE EMPTY BOXES EVERYWHERE.

Ancient Egyptians were the original crazy cat ladies. A number of their deities took feline form, perhaps none more famously than Bastet, who was widely venerated as the goddess of protection and fertility. Ancient artifacts depict Bastet with the body of a woman and the head of a domesticated cat, and her many shrines were filled with kitty-themed offerings, including bronze cat figurines and (gulp) piles of mummified cats.

How to ...
make the perfect
CAT TOY

1. LEAVE YOUR PLATE ON THE TABLE.

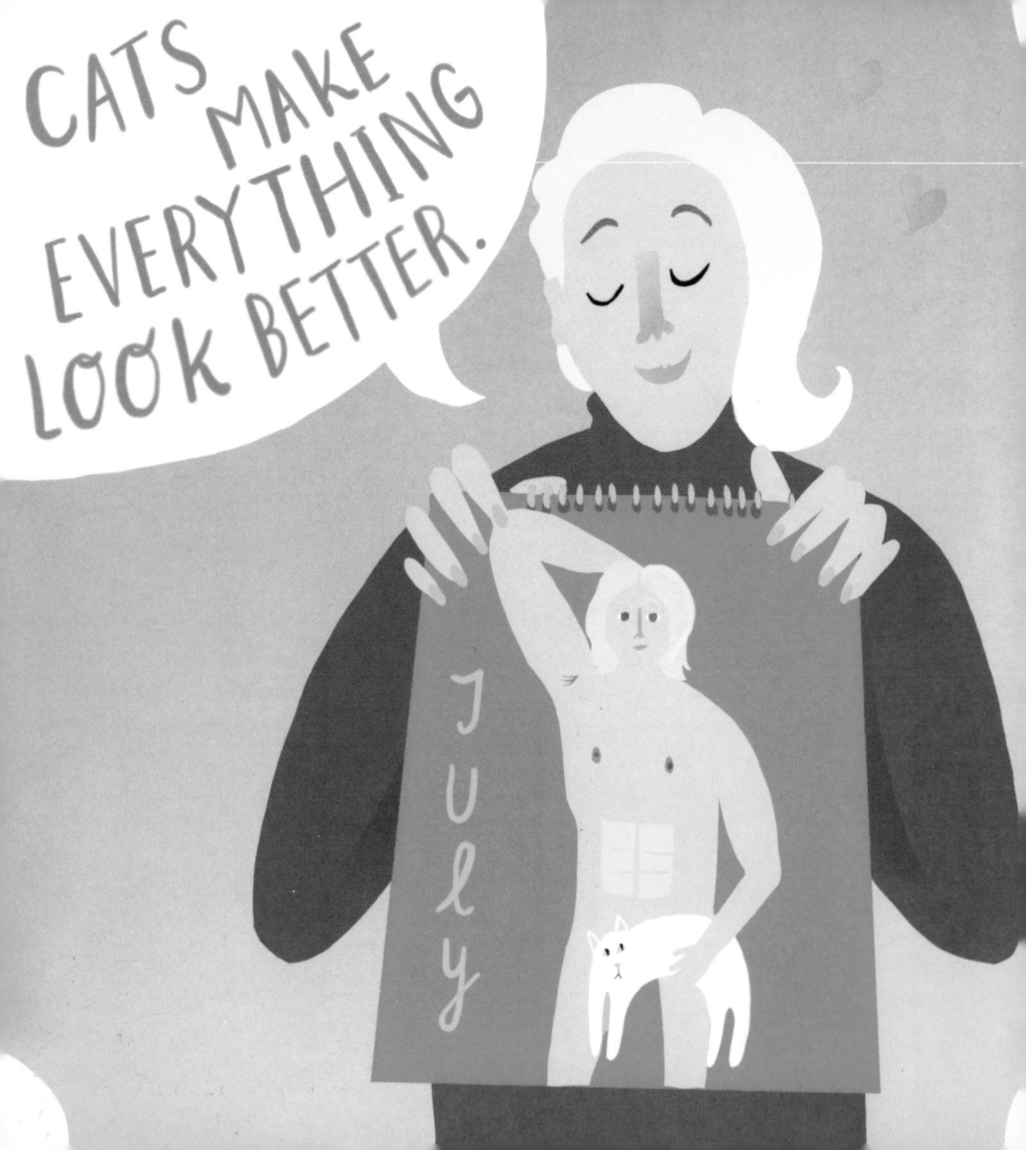
CATS MAKE EVERYTHING LOOK BETTER.
July

Did you know?

Owning a cat could reduce your risk of a heart attack by nearly one third.

Happiness
is only
real when
shared.

How to
DRAW a cat

1.

2.

3.

eraser

4.

Fun fact:
A cat has 230
bones in its body.

Is your cat CUTE?
YES
NO
How is that even possible? ALL CATS ARE CUTE! But okay, let's move on to the next question.
Does the world need to find out all about how amazing your cat is?
Obviously
NO
SURE?
YES
NO
Start that account! Best idea ever!
#crazycatlady
#catscatscats
#purrfect
NOPE!
Forget about this silly idea. Just enjoy the company of your furry friend.
#nohashtagneeded

This is
my happy
place.

CAT HAIR, DON'T CARE.

YOUR SHARED INTEREST . . .

CHASING THAT
3:00 A.M. MOSQUITO.

YOU KNOW YOU'RE A **CRAZY CAT LADY** WHEN...

you start to miss your cat when you're on vacation.

HOW to GROW A CATNIP GARDEN

1 Buy catnip seeds.

2 Plant seeds directly in your garden during spring.

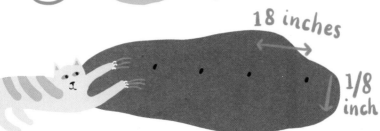

18 inches

1/8 inch

3 Make sure to protect the seedlings from your cat, who will want to lie on top of them!

BAMBOO

CATNIP
(NEPETA CATARIA)
TYPE OF MINT PLANT WITH A CHEMICAL COMPOUND THAT IS VERY ATTRACTIVE TO CATS AND, WHEN CONSUMED, HAS A EUPHORIC EFFECT.

5 If you plant catnip in a pot, you'll probably need to transplant it into a bigger vessel at some point.

4 Water them well during the first few days.
After that, once a week is enough.

6 Let your cat enjoy!

purrrr!

fancy synonyms for CAT lovers

CRAZY CAT LADY

CAT MOM

CAT enthusiast

CAT Addict

Philo Felist

AILUROPHILE

Philo galist

About the Authors

Agnes Loonstra is a freelance illustrator who has worked with a variety of international publications, including *Flow* magazine. Ester Scholten is an educator and writer with a passion for creativity and innovation. They are both self-proclaimed crazy cat ladies, and also unrelated doppelgängers who met each other by chance and became good friends. They live with their cats in the Netherlands.

CRAZY
CAT LADY

You've
CAT
to be
KITTEN
me right
MEOW

CAT HAIR
DON'T CARE